REMEMBER

*Jim & Jean Murr in 1969
Married 25 years*

**By James Murr and
Donna McAndrews**

**Avid Readers Publishing Group
Lakewood, California**

The opinions expressed in this manuscript are those of the authors and do not represent the thoughts or opinions of the publisher. The authors warrant and represent that they have the legal right to publish or own all material in this book. If you find a discrepancy, contact the publisher at www.avidreaderspg.com.

Remembering Jean's Greatest Gift
Living happily at home with Alzheimer's

All Rights Reserved

Copyright © 2010 James Murr and Donna McAndrews

This book may not be transmitted, reproduced, or stored in part or in whole by any means without the express written consent of the publisher except for brief quotations in articles and reviews.

Avid Readers Publishing Group

http://www.avidreaderspg.com

ISBN-13: 978-1-935105-88-6

Printed in the United States

CONTENTS

Introduction: Why the book was written

Part 1 Tapestry..1-8
    Jean Hinkle Murr's biography...Jean's introduction to Jim Murr

Part 2 Ribbons and Bows..9-13
    Jean Murr: wife, mother, friend, hostess

Part 3 Linens and Lace..14-21
    Bearing illness

Part 4 Patchwork Quilt...22-41
    How Jean and Jim Murr and their team managed the caregiving...How others can succeed

Part 5 Rainbow..42-48
    Jean's final days...Jean's passing...a proposal...a special book

Part 6 Mosaic of Practical Matters...................................44-53
    Rearranging the home...Hospice care...Safety...Scheduling...Hiring of employees

Part 7 Stained Glass..54-62
    Financial considerations...lessons learned...finding the proper help...the main caregiver...Jean's greatest gift...Jean's favorite hymn

Memorable Quotes..63-65

The First and Last Extra Mile..66
    Letter from Jim Murr

ACKNOWLEDGEMENTS

By Jim Murr

Without the quality caregivers I had, I could not have even considered being involved in helping to write this book because there would be no success story on which to report.

My profound thanks to my two daughters, Susan Murr and Kathy Alexander. Also Ruth Suttles, Jean's companion and caregiver for seven years, Pam and Alicia Johnson, Renee Gaub, our Hospice team, friends and relatives, all who helped us have a rapid response team available any time of the day or night as needed

These people made up the team which did the daily caring and, I believe, kept Jean alert and happy for many years. To their credit, I am able to help write this book.

Grateful thanks to Therese Everson for her cover design and editorial and technical assistance.

A special thank you to Rick Windsor, an editor who is Jean's nephew, for his technical assistance, editing, feedback and wise suggestions, which kept us inspired and enabled us to complete the book.

INTRODUCTION

By Donna McAndrews

As a family friend, I was honored to be asked by Jim to provide input into the story about Jim and Jean's life in later years, when Jim was challenged with the care of his wife Jean, who suffered from Alzheimer's.

This book is being written not by a member of the medical profession but by a husband who lovingly cared for his wife at home, keeping her happy, calm and contented, in spite of her Alzheimer's disease. Never viewing his role as a hardship, he managed to keep himself happy as well.

This is the story of Jean and Jim Murr. This is a success story. Yes, it's true, the story does end in death, as it will for all of us. But it is what happens between birth and death which is important. So, this is very much a success story. This is the remembering of Jean's greatest gift.

This book was written, not purely as an Alzheimer's "how-to" book, but to let the reader know how we did it, and to let you know that you too can do it with the right set of circumstances, help and the right attitude. Living with Alzheimer's does not have to be a joyless experience, quite the contrary.

You will likely find joy in an unexpected recognition, a loving gesture from another time and, not least, joy in knowing you kept your loved one safe and at peace in a familiar, secure and loving environment.

"This story has so much to offer. To quote from a book by Dr. Linda Morrison Combs, the title being "A Long Goodbye and Beyond", this has truly been 'A Long Goodbye'; after all, what's the hurry to say goodbye?"
Jim Murr

Thousands of books have been written from a clinical perspective, helping people determine if they or their loved one have Alzheimer's, how the disease progresses, what questions to ask the doctors, and many other medical issues. Valuable web sites are also available such as: www.alz.org

This book will not revisit previously documented medical issues but, rather, is designed for one who already has a medical diagnosis of Alzheimer's. It will describe how one man, with the help of family, friends and caregivers, provided for the needs of his wife at home for many years. Further, it will show you how you can do the same for a loved one.

The caregiver, Jim Murr, did not intend for this to be a "love story," but, in fact, it is about a sixty-three year old story of love given, love received and love returned. "The initial infatuation never did diminish in all those sixty-three years," Jim said. Jim believes that this country will soon be seeing the return of a practice that was common in decades past—taking care of loved ones at home throughout the dying process. It is part of the solution of meeting the needs of the Alzheimer's patient. Help is available to you if you intend to be a caregiver and this book can assist you in finding help.

"Patients don't forget true love. I watched Jean's eyes follow Jim in and out of the room." Ruth Suttles, Jean's friend and caregiver for seven years.

TAPESTRY

There is a time for every occupation under heaven: A time for giving birth…
Ecclesiastes 3:1

1921

By Jim Murr and Donna McAndrews

Born at home November fourth in a small town of Nokomis, Illinois, about eighty miles east of St. Louis, Jean grew up in a community with genuine southern hospitality.

Jean's brother, Charles, was eight years older than Jean. Two brothers were born in between Jean and Charles. They both died at childbirth. The term "Blue Babies" was used at the time as to the cause of death. It was not unusual for male "Blue Babies" to die at birth.

Because Jean was a female, she was a healthy and robust survivor. God had a plan for her. She always remembered her happy childhood. Their home was a comfortable bungalow that met their needs and always had room for company. When we would visit, there was always a place for us. Jean's mother was an exceptional house keeper as well as an outstanding cook.

Jean had fond memories of going to Sunday school class, during which time her father was a deacon. Jean remained close to her parents throughout their lives. Shortly after Jean's parent, Minnie and Bob were married, Minnie's mother moved in with the newlyweds. She was a very pleasant but dependent person. She just didn't have any other place where she was welcome to stay. She very seldom ventured off the homestead. Jean's mother was the oldest of five children and it fell to her to take care of their mother. Her mother stayed for over fifty years and she died at their home. This may have set an example for future generations to follow. Jean's father and mother, Jim's mother, two grandmothers, two grandfathers and a step grandfather all died at home. My conclusion is that you get out of a family relationship what you put into it.

Bob, Jean's father, did electrical maintenance for the New York Central Railroad for over fifty years. They were able to survive the Great Depression by Bob being good at what he did and being willing to work in all kinds of weather in order to help keep the railroad running. He loved the railroad.

Bob was well thought of throughout the railroad system. He was so well liked that he was actually given a five-year extension beyond the normal retirement age, thus working on the railroad for 51 years!

Bob would have worked beyond that time, but it was feared he might be a danger to himself with active train tracks. For a time, the railroad did assign him a young man to help with the climbing tasks and some of the painting. The railroad was very good to Bob.

The family didn't own an automobile until 1936 but Bob's territory was close to home so he was able to walk to work. The grocery store was also close to home and Bob was able to walk home for lunch, if he was working nearby that day.

High School & Beyond
1939 to 1946
By Donna McAndrews

In the "Old Nokomis" yearbook of 1939, proof is to be found of Jean's chief characteristics, repeated over and over again by her many friends in high school: neat, friendly and one of the school's best dressers, thanks to her mother being a seamstress.

One of her most frequent expressions as printed beside her senior-year picture was "What did I forget, Rose?" Rose was none other than Jean's best friend. She was also referred as one of the "tall girls," a "giggler" and "one of the nicest looking girls in the entire high school."

Yearbook picture 1939

ROSALEE M. McKINNEY
"Be ready early, Jean."

JEAN E. HINKLE
"What did I forget, Rose?"

A popular section in any high school yearbook is the "senior will." In Jean's senior year, she "willed" her "peaches and cream complexion to anyone who needs it."

Jeanie was her nickname and her hobby was written as "arguing." Again, her most prominent characteristic was "neatness" and her ambition was modeling; it was also believed that she could have a future as an orator.

only six boys — you look the best of girls!!

Class Reunion Of 1939

The Class of 1939 held their reunion Sept. 8 at the Gardens in Litchfield. Attending front row from left are, Athanasis (Jaros)Lowder, Lena (Conterio) Davito and Dorothy (Holmes) Downs.
In the second row are Alvin Beaman, Lois (Schneider) Jostes, Doris (Battles) Stanbery, Delores (Boyd) Peters, Lucille (Berns) Butkauskas, Charlotte (Nash) Green, Jean (Hickle) Murr and Ossie Pretner.
In the back row are Vic Jostes, Loren Ruppert, Louise (Wolf) Singler, C. F. Marley, Iola (Johnson) McKittick and Jay Stiehl.

Class Of 1941 Honors Deceased Classmates

As the Nokomis Township High School Class of 1941 celebrates their 60th high school reunion they remember and honor their deceased members: Edward Bald, Henry Boyd, Louis Brotsmeyer, Dale Browning, Cecil Carroll, Anna Forgacs, Rosie (Dezelak) Gasprich, Ruth (Hoff) Rosche, Ann (Jachino) Price, Jennie (Jachino) Berra, Edwin Johnson, Vernon Johnson, Josephine Kalvitis, Mary Ellen (Kelly) Johnson, Mike Kosko, and Lavada (Krutaki) Hager.
Also, Edna Lehenbauer, Wilbur Lewey, Lester Livingston, William Nash, Robert Peel, Thomas Poliak, Florence (Rhodes) Mitchell, Charles Rupert, Lillian (Ryan) Kansey, Jean (Schaefer) Vercellotti, William Schaefer, Virginia (Schroeder) Phipps, George Sneddon, Eugene Stoltz, Robert Watne, Lloyd Williams and Paul Zimmerman.

CALL THE FP-P
563-2115

Jean is second from right in the Nokomis, IL Newspaper

Jean graduated from high school and then moved to Peoria, Illinois where she lived with her aunt; there Jean went to business school. During this time, she contracted scarlet fever. Her parents and her brother picked her up to bring her home and, on the way home, they had a terrible automobile accident.

After the accident, Jean's mother Minnie was disabled for the rest of her life but, not to the extent that she couldn't take care of herself and her home.

When Minnie died, the accident from years ago was determined to be the cause of death but, she lived to 87 so other things were probably wrong with her too.

At this time, Jean was engaged to a young man who was in the Army during World War II. It was during the African campaign that he was killed. This, of course, was a low point in her life.

Soon after, Jean decided to go to Chicago to live

with a friend, a young woman from Jean's hometown, and her friend's baby. Her friend's husband was serving with the Marines in the South Pacific. She found a job and rented space from her friend. Both women were able to live independently since they were ambitious.

Jean worked as a guard in a defense plant and was required to carry a gun. The enemy didn't know what they had here; they had an opportunity to walk right in and take over the place. Jean would never even shoot a mouse, but she did pack her iron and the enemy never really did attack the place, so we'll give her credit for doing her duty, which she would have been good at, even if she didn't have to shoot a gun.

Toward the end of the war, when it was learned that her girlfriend's husband was coming home from the South Pacific, her friend's family planned to move to the town of South St. Paul, Minnesota. Her friend's husband was also a railroad employee and the Minnesota suburb was where he worked before going into the service. The family invited Jean to give Minnesota a try and Jean agreed, although she had heard that a person can be walking down the street in Minnesota and just fall over dead from the cold.

Jean was prepared for the worst when she got off the train after midnight in January 1946. She had to walk three blocks to a windy corner and wait for a streetcar. (This was the time just before the arrival of the city bus.) She proceeded to check the railroad schedule. She was going to get out of here, but quick! Well, her friends convinced her to stick around for a while and she did.

1946
By Jim Murr

I had my life all planned. I was not going to take any girl out on a second date. One date and then move on.

That way, I wouldn't fall by the wayside like all my friends. With this I was firm: no marriage.

But, in the case of my latest date, Jean, with all my friends pestering me about this "new girl," I decided I might as well take this lady out again; I'd never marry that screwball, I had thought to myself.

Now, sixty-two years after marrying Jean, I can laugh at my firm resolve. I know I made the best choice; I hope she did too.

"An open mind leaves a chance for someone to drop a worthwhile thought in it." Phil Jackason

...a time for dancing...Eccl 3:4

Jim – 1946
By Jim Murr

We hung out in the same social circles—men and women just being together nobody was committed. It was Easter Sunday, 1946, and several of the guys and gals were going down to a roadhouse to get something to eat, talk and maybe dance a little. Jean was the "new girl" but she fit in just fine. Jean was a lady who never met a stranger.

As Jean and I were sitting at the bar, time went by and I wanted to buy her a drink. However, I had no money because I had to spend all my discharge money to repair a car that I had damaged by running into the side of a moving freight train (with a blonde, no less.) At any rate, she loaned me $10 so I could buy her a drink and a couple for myself, of course. This was quite amazing because $10 was a week's wages in 1946.

However, Jean announced, "This man will pay me back!"

...a time for planting...a time for building...Eccl 3:2-3

RIBBONS AND BOWS

...a time for laughter...Eccl 3:4

"Jean's eyes tell a million things. She was my friend for sixteen years. She always gave me the best answers." Renee Gaub

"We loved the "Ozzie and Harriet" existence of Jean and Jim after we moved to town in 1968. My sister and I nearly tripped each other getting to her door to taste any of her baking." Friend and neighbor, Mary Muller

The Domestic Jean

Jean's beautiful, immaculate home was the center of her universe, agreed Jean's daughters, Susan and Kathy. Their mom grew up in a simpler time when a woman's family and home were her main priorities.

Sitting at the kitchen table just before Christmas 2009, Sue was making the most beautiful, huge bows in red and green ribbon. "These are Jean's bows," Sue said. "Mom taught me how to make them." One of Jean's many "trademarks."

Jean was the greatest caregiver and nurturer, according to her daughters, also a good judge of human nature and totally dedicated to husband and family.

Susan and Kathy recalled that they were raised Catholic, their father's religion and attended Catholic school when young. Jean, a non-Catholic, volunteered as a playground attendant for three years. The Catholic nuns who taught at the school never realized that Jean wasn't Catholic. When portraying to the students one day how a "good Catholic mother" would act, one of the Sisters used Jean as an example.

Jean also worked with a group of women at a newly established hospital in South St. Paul. After years of volunteerism there, Jean received a Papal Blessing, even though she was the only non-Catholic in the group.

"Jean loved it when people ate...and ate a lot! She enjoyed attending high school reunions in Nokomis. She was fun loving and zany at times. We all loved her." Steve Hinkle, Jean's nephew

"People loved to touch and hug Jean because, for one thing, she always smelled so good." Mary Muller.

Clean Jean

A great pride of Jean's was a sparkling clean home. Besides this, laundry was always hung, never machinedried. Floors were scrubbed on hands and knees, cookies were home-baked and there would be no latchkey situation for Jean's family. And then there were Jean's famous desserts.

When getting together with family—children, brothers, sisters, in-laws, grandchildren, 29 cousins—everyone requested Jean to bring the desserts. Kathy and Sue especially remember their mom's chocolate icebox dessert, prayer bars, blueberry dessert and lemon bars to name a few; Jean didn't scrimp on desserts.

"She lived a good life because she was a good person, a loveable person. She had something spiritual to give from within her; she enriched us all." Rick Gellman, friend

"Jean was a real lady, she was never critical, she had wonderful values. She didn't need to talk about them because she lived them daily." Sue Windsor, Jean's niece

Crowning Glory

Those close to Jean knew her hair was very important to her and she always kept it just so, retaining her natural color. Her hair always remained thick and full and she preferred a curly style.

There was one exception when Jean was forced to "go straight." During one of the three times Jim and Jean vacationed in the Virgin Islands, while riding in a boat, a large wave caught the boat and Jean's hair. Jean was forced to "go native" and live with straight hair for a time. She was a good sport about it; as always she was able to laugh at herself.

"Jean always kept her happy personality. She was known for delivering her 'Gracie Allen' one-liner-type quips and her 'Yogi Berra' responses." Husband, Jim Murr

Model of Hospitality

A story was told by Tom Murr, Jean's nephew, of when, on one occasion, he visited Jim and Jean. Jim and Tom were in the breezeway area and Jean was busy, as usual, in the kitchen. Jean called cheerily to Jim, "Hon, do you want a sandwich?" "No thanks, hon" came a sweet reply.

A short while later, this same question and answer repeated itself in the same sweet tone...and then a third time! Jean continued scurrying about in the kitchen and shortly appeared with a sandwich for her beloved husband. Said Jim to his visitor when Jean exited, "I really wanted that sandwich; I just didn't want two."

Tom Murr's father had come for a visit when Jean called to the men: "Would you like a glass of iced tea?" The answer was negative. Then, "Would you like a cup of coffee?" Same answer. Finally, "Do you want some wine?" Neither man did, but Jean was not put off.

Jean came scurrying in with big tumblers. Before long, the tongue of Tom's Dad seemed to thicken and his speech slurred a bit. "What is this?" the men asked. "Well, said Jean, its whiskey; you didn't want wine!"

"Aunt Jean was a model of hospitality, a living sermon. She would bring—at the very least—a cup of coffee to every visitor." Tom Murr, nephew

"I delighted in Jean, even in her frail health. She had a smile and a twinkle and she could put words together in unique and remarkable ways, even at a time when words were not coming to her—like the time she said to me (during advanced Alzheimer's)—'Thank you for coming!' just as clear as could be." Hospice Chaplain, Norman Belland

Believe in Beauty

Pam Johnson first met the Murrs when she moved into a mobile home in Healy Park. The home had been cherished by Helen Healy, Jim Murr's Mother who was also the park developer and who had lived there for thirty years. Pam became Jean's companion and caregiver for many years.

"When I first met Jean we connected at once. When she smiled at me I could feel warmth in her heart and she became a blessing to me.

"As time went by, Jean would say things that were beyond funny. For example, her breakfast of bran cereal she called 'gruel.' Whenever I brought it to her she'd say, 'Oh brother', and she'd roll her eyes and laugh. She was a joy to be around.

"Jean was a strong willed person with a tender heart that warmed everyone; her smile was like the sunshine and her eyes sparkled like diamonds.

"Another joy in my life is my daughter Alisha, who is now 13. Jean loved my daughter and brought many smiles to her face. Alisha adored Jean and helped care for her. Jean was a great hugger. She would squeeze and hug you in a way that said, 'don't leave'.

"One day I was helping Jean pick out a dress for Jim's birthday party. She said a firm 'no' to every outfit I showed her until I came to the special one she wanted. Only that one would do.

LINENS AND LACE
The Human Condition: Bearing Illness
…a time for healing… Eccl 3:3

Bearing Illness 1969 Onward
By Jim Murr

Jean and I were traveling on a summer vacation and she seemed insistent that when we got back to town the two of us would go to the Mayo Clinic in Rochester for a good physical for me.

I felt there was no apparent reason for this, but agreed to go as long as Jean would get a physical also.

After a thorough examination, I was told by doctors that if I didn't change my ways of living I wouldn't be alive at age fifty-five. I was forty-five at the time.

I thought that this seemed to be in line with family problems of heart disease and strokes and these problems being brought about by – not wild living – but living beyond one's ability to absorb it.

I must have done something right, because it's now 2010; I'm 85 years of age, and on my fourth doctor at the Mayo Clinic.

Jean was examined and a large polyp was found on her colon; the doctor said it was the size of a grapefruit. This seemed incredible but it was a very real probability that she might have to go through life with a colostomy bag. Yet, this was taken care of and Jean returned to health for the time being.

Starting with the early onset of migraines in her youth, Jean's medical history was marked with a variety of misfortunes and setbacks that would have stopped most people. Jean would always amaze us with her comeback-style of handling adverse medical problems. Nothing ever set her back for very long; she was able to adjust and move on.

1989
By Jim Murr

"Help, help, help" are the startling words I heard when returning home one day about twenty years ago.

After searching downstairs, upstairs and downstairs

again, I found the answer. In the newly installed shower stall was Jean. She was shivering from the cold and crying out of frustration. This was the first time she had used the newly installed shower and she could not figure out how to open the door to get out.

For two days afterward, Jean had a migraine headache, but, later, she would laugh along with everyone else when we spoke of "mom's latest funny event." This helped form Jean's Gracie Allen-type reputation.

Was the above an early sign of Alzheimer's disease? No one knows for sure. "

With any dementia, the brain and hands no longer work together." Author Unknown

Don't Quit

When things go wrong, as they sometimes will
When the road you're trudging seems all uphill
When the funds are low and the debts are high
And you want to smile, but you have to sigh
When care is pressing you down a bit
Rest if you must, but don't you quit.

Life is queer with its twists and turns
As every one of us sometimes learns
And many a fellow turns about
When he might have won, had he stuck it out.
Don't give up though the pace seems slow
You may succeed with another blow.

Often the goal is nearer than
It seems to a faint and faltering man;
Often the struggler has given up
When he learned too late when the night came down
How close he was to the golden crown.

Success is failure turned inside out
The silver tint of the clouds of doubt
And you never can tell how close you are

It may be near when it seems afar;
So stick to the fight when you're hardest hit
It's when things seem worst that you mustn't quit.
-**Author Unknown**

The above motivation poem was sent to Jean and Jim by an MGFA member after Jean was diagnosed with Myasthenia Gravis, one of many illnesses Jean was able to overcome because she didn't know what it meant to give up.

Never did Jean complain about having Alzheimer's, although we discussed her illness openly on many occasions. Her medical history includes three small strokes, tripping accidents, falls, poor medical advice, broken bones and two internal operations.

It seems that Alzheimer's was the only thing she couldn't fight off. The nine years between diagnosis and death were all good and enjoyable years because of her outstanding spirit.

When Jean suffered a slight stroke and a subsequent hip replacement, she was moved to a nursing home for therapy. I knew the moment I took her to the nursing home that she would not be there alone. I arranged for someone to be with her 24 hours a day. The good news for me was that I found out about the operation of nursing homes through this experience. I made the decision then that there was no circumstance—providing I was alive—that Jean was ever going to be put in a nursing home alone again. That began the idea that there was a better way to care for a loved one in need of care. Jean asked me at that time if I would take care of her if the need arose. The only honest answer I could give was that I was not the caregiver type, but would gladly give her care for as long as necessary.

When Jean came home, we had more problems. Jean went to a hockey game in a snowstorm to see our son. I had advised her not to go. She fell and broke her wrist, requiring another cast, another operation and more anesthetic. I wondered aloud if some of Jean's later problems could be attributed to putting her to sleep so many times. Could anesthesia even trigger Alzheimer's?

In 1994 both Jean and I were defendants in a civil law suit filed against us. We were both called to give evidence as we knew it. Each of us was allowed to sit in on the questioning of the other. Jean was questioned first and became confused about dates and events, so I needed to intervene and halt the questioning.

At that time her myasthenia gravis was quite active; fatigue and some confusion were possible side effects of the disease. The opposing attorney excused Jean from any further questions. Again, could this have been Alzheimer's? It is very possible since, shortly thereafter, the M.G. caused no more problems.

The above mentioned court case was a fabrication and the judge's finding was completely in our favor; we were awarded a judgment we had not even asked for!

In 2001, we went to the Mayo Clinic. Daughter Sue had thought mom was being anxious for no reason. This was when they said Jean had Alzheimer's. The doctor advised that her driver's license be revoked.

I was in denial about the driving because Jean had driven the 80 miles to the Mayo Clinic, all freeway driving, then into the parking ramp and parked the car before waking me up; I had slept all the way. Jean was an absolutely excellent driver. She continued to drive for two more years without a permit—no accidents, no tickets.

Many times Jean had driven me up to our cabin in the Itasca Park area of Minnesota. Our place was 240 miles away. She did exceptionally well as a driver.

Eventually, I removed myself from all the businesses I had been involved with and took more time to stay home and do what Jean and I often had talked about: retirement. This left me always available to drive if Jean needed to go someplace. Jean never complained once about phasing out her driving; it just happened naturally.

The purpose of this chapter, in addition to narrating health and healing issues, is also to comment on the medications that doctors prescribe.

Over the years, Jean accumulated a supply of drugs

doctors had given her but never discontinued. As her Alzheimer's progressed, it seemed she was getting worse, even hallucinating. She began seeing things at night. Upon Jean's request, I would get up and clear the people she was seeing out of the house. When Jean started to wander, I was worried she might get out of the house with no one there to help her, so I purchased extra locks for all the doors.

At this time, a close friend of mine and all three of our children—Jimmy, Sue and Kathy—within a few days of one another, all said, "We think mom is overmedicated." It never dawned on me as a "dumb plumber" that this could happen. This was a dilemma.

Rather than go back to the six or seven doctors and quiz them all, I wondered if the medication was the culprit. Was it the medication that was not allowing Jean to keep food down and the resulting dehydration? Jean went from 129 pounds to 96 pounds because she just couldn't eat or drink. For a couple of days, I discontinued the medicines—one hundred percent. (None of these medicines were the day-to-day, essential-to-life medications.)

After a short time, I introduced back into her regimen the pills that had never caused side effects: aspirin, heart medicine, etc. As other pills were gradually added on a daily basis, Jean's symptoms recurred, including hallucinations and vomiting. Thereafter, I discontinued these pills, one at a time, until I had problem medications isolated. The result was that Jean quit wandering and hallucinating. In addition her appetite came back. I gave her a couple of "Boost" or "Ensure" each day, along with good meals. When she was able to eat again, she was soon up to 118 pounds. This was like a small miracle; she was no longer a bag of bones. She was putting on weight and looking healthier.

I won't mention the names of the medicines which caused Jean problems since other people might do well with them and get good results. I advise everyone to read about all side effects, and then reread them, and read them a third time. If a person has the problems that appear in the warnings, it's time to take action. Don't depend on the drug companies to help you out; check it out for yourself to avoid suffering side effects. It is the caregiver's responsibility to check every medicine.

Pills can become a way of life. People think they have to have a certain medication every day or they will die. In some cases, however, it may be the medicine causing the illness or death.

I am proud of the fact that, to the present day, I never had to install those extra locks on the doors; Jean stopped wandering.

A Lesson Learned

I learned what can happen at a nursing home even when a family member stays with the patient.

When Jean had been sent by her doctor to a nearby nursing home for physical therapy, I was with her day and night. She received two treatments each day, so we had about twenty-two hours every day with nothing to do.

On a Friday which was the third day of Jean's scheduled treatment, her therapist announced that she was taking a long weekend from work; Jean would not be having an afternoon treatment that day. Since the coming Monday was a holiday, Jean's next treatment would not be until Tuesday afternoon of the following week. I knew that my protesting this unacceptable schedule wouldn't be addressed until the following week. I believed that taking Jean home would be best for Jean and me.

Therefore, I wheeled Jean back to her room, picked up her belongings, and went to the check-out desk. The nurse in charge told me I couldn't leave with Jean. I told her if she wanted to stop me she would have to call the police and, if he arrived in time, he could help me get Jean from the wheel chair into our car. Out the door we went. We encountered no problems and no police.

By the time we got home we had plenty of help. The word had spread that Dad sprung Mom from the nursing home and plenty of help showed up. I wonder how much this saved Medicare. Jean recovered just fine at home.

Maximizing Opportunities

Janice Farr of Derby, Kansas, was one of Jean's favorite nieces; she happens to be a retired nurse with many years of experience. After Jean's diagnosis of Alzheimer's, niece Janice would call often out of concern for Jean and offer good, professional advice.

About two years before Jean died, Janice was at our home for a visit. Together with our family doctor, our two daughters and niece Janice, we decided to apply for Medicare Stay-at-Home Hospice service for Jean. The normal start-up service would be three home-care visits per week from Hospice caregivers, plus a weekly visit from Kathy, a Hospice nurse.

Because of the fact that I had waited a longer time to seek outside help than I might have, Jean's condition had advanced to a point at which she now qualified for five Hospice visits per week. This amounted to a forty percent increase in care for Jean because niece Janice was knowledgeable about progression of Alzheimer's disease and knew we needed more help at that time. Thanks to Janice knowing that this extra help was available, we were able to keep Jean at home.

PATCHWORK QUILT

"Jim brought a calming presence to Jean. To him, nothing was a problem, only a challenge."   Donna McAndrews

HOW WE DID IT

Making Home a Place of Peace and Comfort

By Jim Murr

This part of the book will describe what we did as a team of caregivers to meet the needs of our patient, Jean Murr. All of us realize that quality of life is important, not necessarily longevity; it happened that Jean and I were able to have both quality and longevity.

Jean and I were able to handle and cope with Alzheimer's very successfully. Perhaps this is unheard of, but the approach we used was successful. Consider that Jean awoke with a smile every morning. This is hard for me to do every day and I don't have Alzheimer's.

Jean was diagnosed with Alzheimer's in 2001 by the Mayo Clinic. My children recently told me they discussed mom's Alzheimer's problems ten years before that. If they discussed it with me, I have no recollection of it but the important thing was, they recognized a problem.

The early stages of the disease are not hard to manage and handle. In fact, it is so relatively simple that it fools a lot of people into thinking, "Heck, I can handle this to the end." This may be true if it's an early end but if the disease spans many years, it's a long journey, not necessarily a bad journey, an unusual journey; it just takes time to complete.

From what I've seen and what I have been personally involved with, it is extremely important that you intervene early and assertively for both your own behalf and that of the patient.

The early stages of Alzheimer's are very deceiving. Patients can still function; they are able to do ninety percent of what they always did, and you can be lulled into the idea that this is as bad as it gets. Well, it isn't, and by the time most people are diagnosed, they are so overwhelmed that they just can't handle it. Many people I know didn't lay out a course to follow and it rained disaster after disaster. What

I hope to tell you is what worked for us.

Are all stages the same? Will this advice help everyone? Probably not. But let's pick a number: I believe forty percent would be successful if they follow my plan.

One thing to consider is that compared to the present methods of handling the disease billions of dollars would be saved. In my opinion tens of thousands of jobs would be created to deal with this medical issue alone. But the main consideration is the quality of life which you seldom hear about for the Alzheimer's patient. This could all be accomplished within the funding already being used to treat Alzheimer's disease.

Checking the House for Potential Problems

The first thing to do, if you have a loved one with Alzheimer's, is to take a good look at your home and make it "kid proof" in a sense. Get rid of throw rugs and get rid of items on the floor that might be difficult to see. Also, try to remove low-lying obstacles such as foot stools, tables, clutter, electrical cords, newspapers and books, etc. which might invite tripping. Prepare to avoid accidents before the fact rather than after. Don't be too proud to put up grab bars where needed. We installed some near the bed and three or four in the bathroom. Put grab bars any place you think people might be able to use them if they should start to stumble. Quite honestly, this saved me more than it did Jean. In all probability this was because her falls and breaks were due to small strokes and this didn't allow her the time to grab onto anything.

The grab bars were a godsend when Jean was getting in and out of the tub and getting up and down for toileting. Another plus is having a grab bar at the front of the vanity while standing at the washbasin. So, swallow your pride and swallow your ego and put up several grab bars.

Personally, I prefer those with a smaller diameter. It seems to me that Jean, with her arthritis, could grip those better and I know I like them better than the larger grab bars, although I used both and they both work. Either way, grab bars will serve you well.

"It's extremely difficult, if not impossible; to be the sole provider for someone with Alzheimer's through the entire course of the disease." <u>Mayo Clinic on Alzheimer's Disease; Mayo Clinic; Rochester, Minnesota; 2002</u>

Jean's care schedule

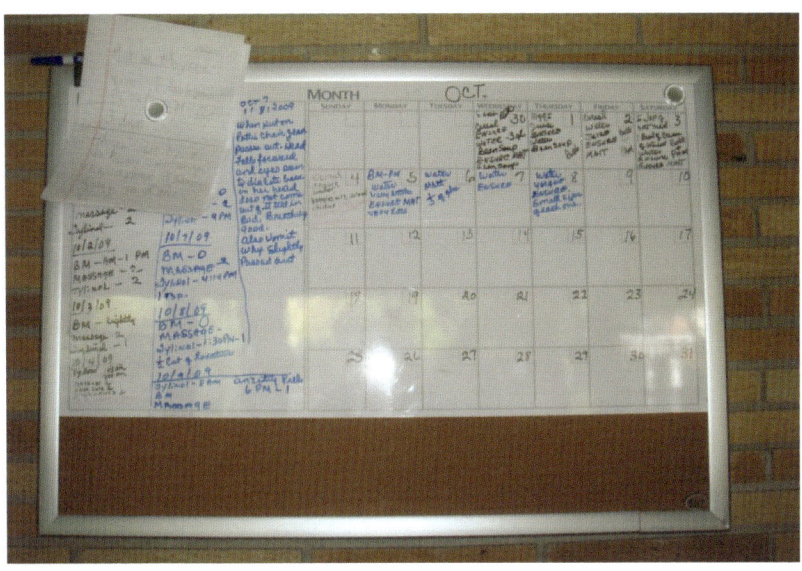

Bathroom with grab bars

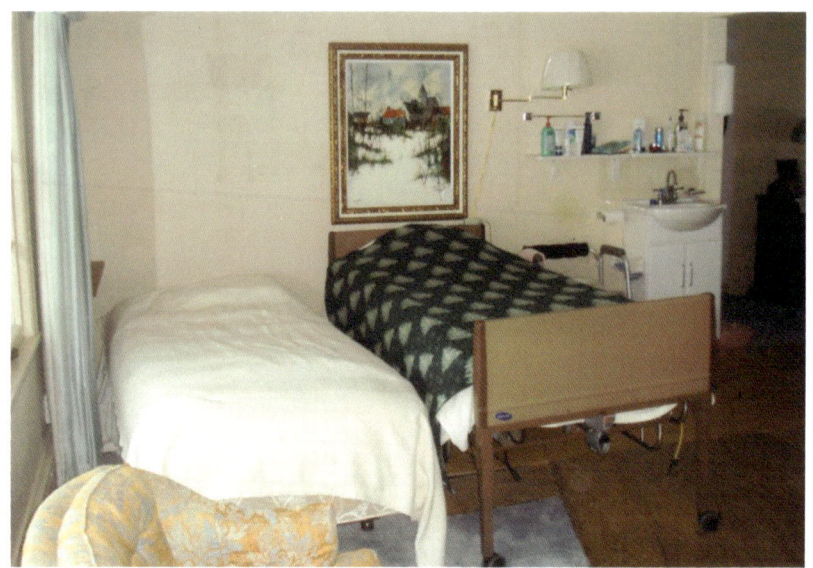

Converted living room with wash basin and protective plywood installed over the carpet

The Bedroom and the Day Room

We had a king-sized bed in our bedroom so there wasn't much space for a wheelchair or a portable toilet or later, a standup lift. We cleared out as much living room furniture as was necessary and we put our bed in the living room. Thus, we had a nice big bedroom which was formerly our living space. Single beds are the only practical way to service a patient who is confined to bed. *(See picture above.)*

In the family room or den, we have a nice picture window and we could enjoy a bright morning. Also, in this room, is the fireplace. A good part of Jean's day was spent in this room, right up until the time she passed away. *(Our family room is pictured below.)*

Moving our beds to the former living room allowed us to care for Jean more easily and also gave Jean a better position so she could enjoy the sunshine and the people in our home going about their tasks. It is a joy to watch when something catches the attention of an Alzheimer's patient which might bring happiness to them. Planned activities are necessary but sometimes unplanned events, such as a surprise visit, will set a pleasant tone for the whole day. This physical contact is so vital, especially when the patient has lost the ability to speak.

With this layout, Jean was always able to be in contact, never losing sight of me or the main caregiver of the time. She certainly became slower and her mind took longer to focus, but you could eventually get through to her and she'd have little bursts of enthusiasm when a person would say something funny.

At bedtime, we were able to lie down close to each other and hold hands, which was very satisfying. This was also a Godsend when Jean was restless and maybe having a nightmare. All I had to do was reach over, touch her, and say, "Jean, wake up and go back to sleep." This worked every time like a miracle drug which cost nothing and had no bad side effects.

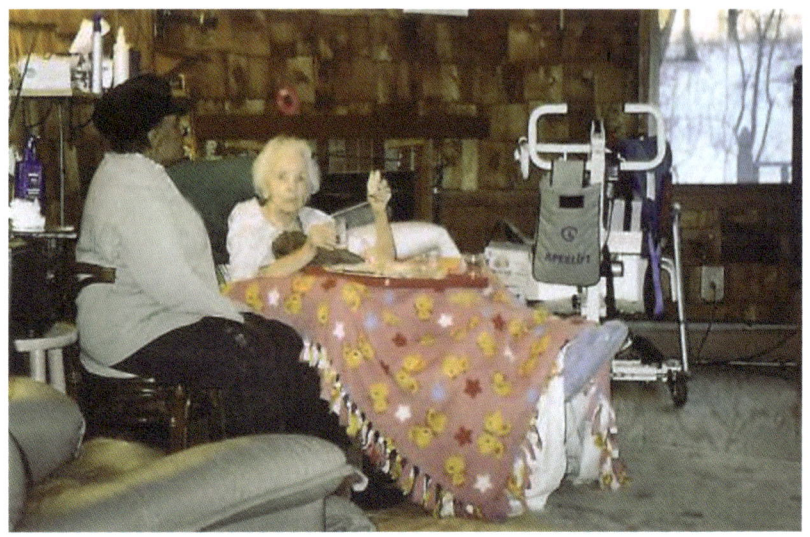

Jean with Ruth, the main caregiver after Jim, in family room

Simplifying

Almost from the beginning of her treatment, after having the information from the Mayo Clinic, I arranged for Jean to have a companion 24 hours a day, seven days a week. For the most part, this companion was me. I curtailed all my activities that I could, closed down some business involvements and Jean and I focused on enjoying life together.

Walkers and Lifts

Eventually Jean needed a walker for stability. One day she did fall over backwards while using the walker but it appeared she had a slight stroke. She hit her head really hard on the radiator and broke a hip again. Back we went to the hospital, where she had her hip pinned.

She pulled through that really well and we were soon back home again.

At this time, I decided to get a stand-up lift which I found in the newspaper classifieds under "used medical equipment". We had not been aware they even existed but the seller demonstrated how he used it. His wife had been in a similar situation. I decided on the spot to buy it and it really extended Jean's mobility. Instead of having to balance herself, she had a kind of harness we were able to put around her. An electric motor takes up the slack under the arms and it supports the patient. All Jean had to do was stand in there; it was on wheels and we could move her. The bottom tray the patient stands on is removable so the patient is able to walk, when walking is possible, and have no fear of falling. The patient is easily transported from one area to the next. This is a wonderful idea and I'm surprised they aren't used more often. I can't say enough about them.

When Jean was in the final stages of Alzheimer's, we needed to begin using a Hoyer lift. This lift is designed in such a way that the patient lies in a hammock-type seat and the weight is distributed a lot better. It is more comfortable for the patient but some mobility is lost when changing from the stand-up lift. We were able to use both to good advantage and we could recommend the lift to anyone not ready for a wheelchair only but having stability problems.

The Flooring

We also needed to make adjustments with the flooring, so we put plywood over carpeting, screwed the plywood to the floor and this made a ramp/runway which allowed Jean's lift to travel easily; otherwise, the wheels, being rather small, tend to get hung up on the carpet, making it difficult to move and it slows down the whole operation. It also requires the patient to remain in the harness longer. It is best to get the patient in and out of the harness as quickly as possible for her comfort.

We applied two coats of shellac on the top side of the plywood. The first coat was thinned so it would penetrate the wood and seal it. The second coat was left thick in order to strengthen the finish. We anticipated some spilling, so these layers of shellac made wiping up faster and also helped control odors and stains. One does not want to wipe the flooring with ammonia; it will leave an odor which smells much like another liquid that has just been wiped up. (The word will soon be on the street that you are a poor caregiver!) Other hard finishes may work just as well but shellac is easy to apply and dries quickly.

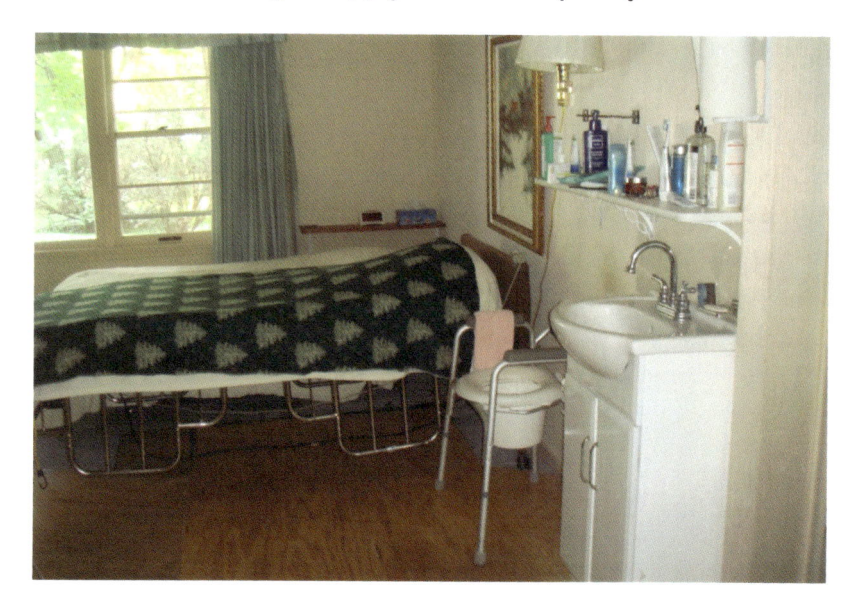

Work station next to Jean's bed

The Wheelchair

Of course, we used the wheel chair quite a bit. It was handy for taking Jean outside in the driveway or to take her down the street to wave to the neighbors and the kids—just to keep the patient in touch with others as much as possible. We enjoyed this activity very much.

Chairs

Before we got the stand-up lift, we used a lift chair which was a comfortable overstuffed, battery-operated chair that stands you up. The chair is a very handy thing to have when getting someone up to put them in a wheelchair. The problem with this was that I couldn't handle her weight long enough to turn her and swing her into a wheelchair, even though she only weighed about 125 pounds. But, being off-balance, we lost her a couple of times and I had to call for help so we could pick her up and put her in the wheelchair. It's nice when it works, but one needs to have a really good grip on the patient and I was not strong enough for the transfer.

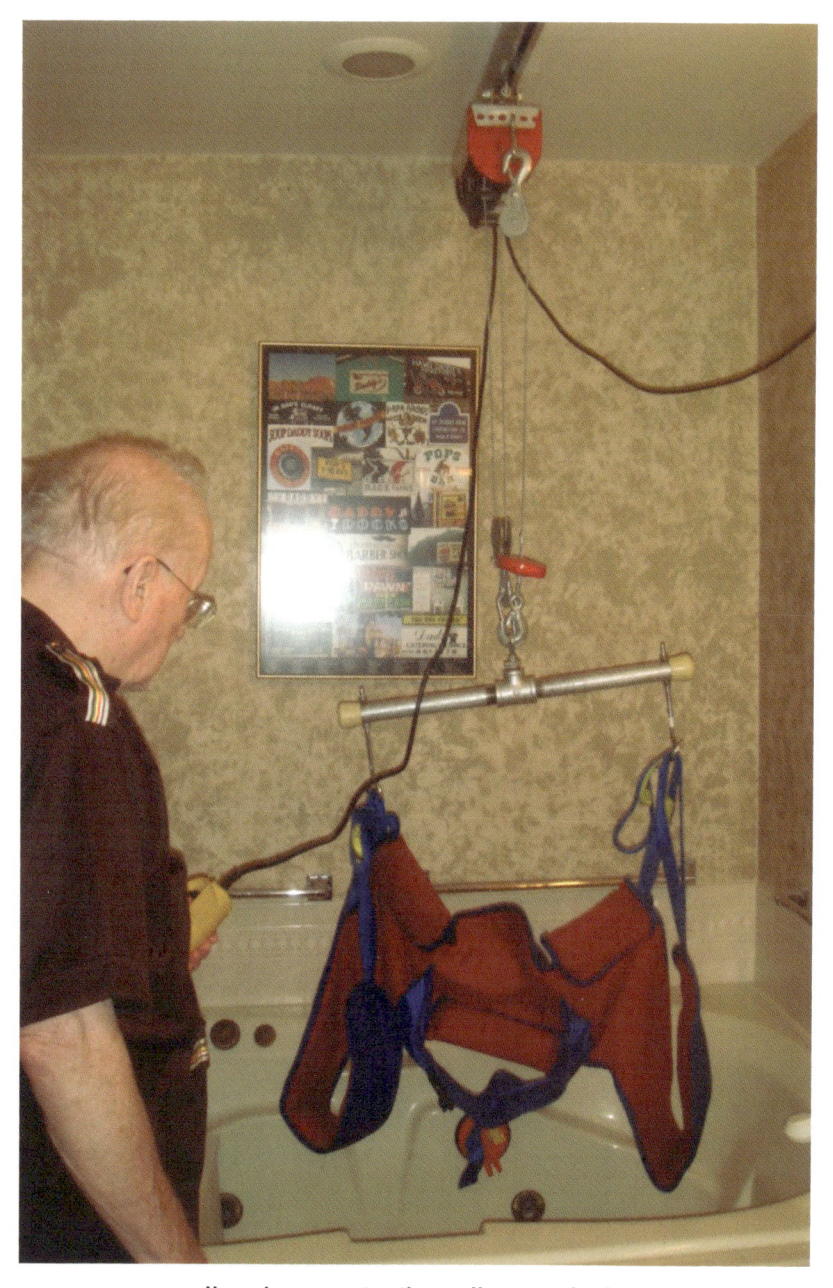

Jim demonstrating sling on hoist

"Even though Jean could no longer walk, talk, or feed herself, she's still the same person." Jim Murr

Murr's pet, Cinnamon

The Overhead Hoist

Another idea that worked really well was taking the harness from the lift and using it in the overhead hoist in the bathroom, where we had a track on the ceiling. Here we were able to pick her up out of her wheelchair and up high enough to clear the edge of the whirlpool tub, swing her over, and lower her into the tub. There she could enjoy her whirlpool. I think it gave her good stimulation and kept her from getting dried out skin. It usually took an extra person in the bathroom for safety purposes, not lifting, to get her in and out. This is one place you want added help to avoid accidents. I recommend this for the comfort of the patient.

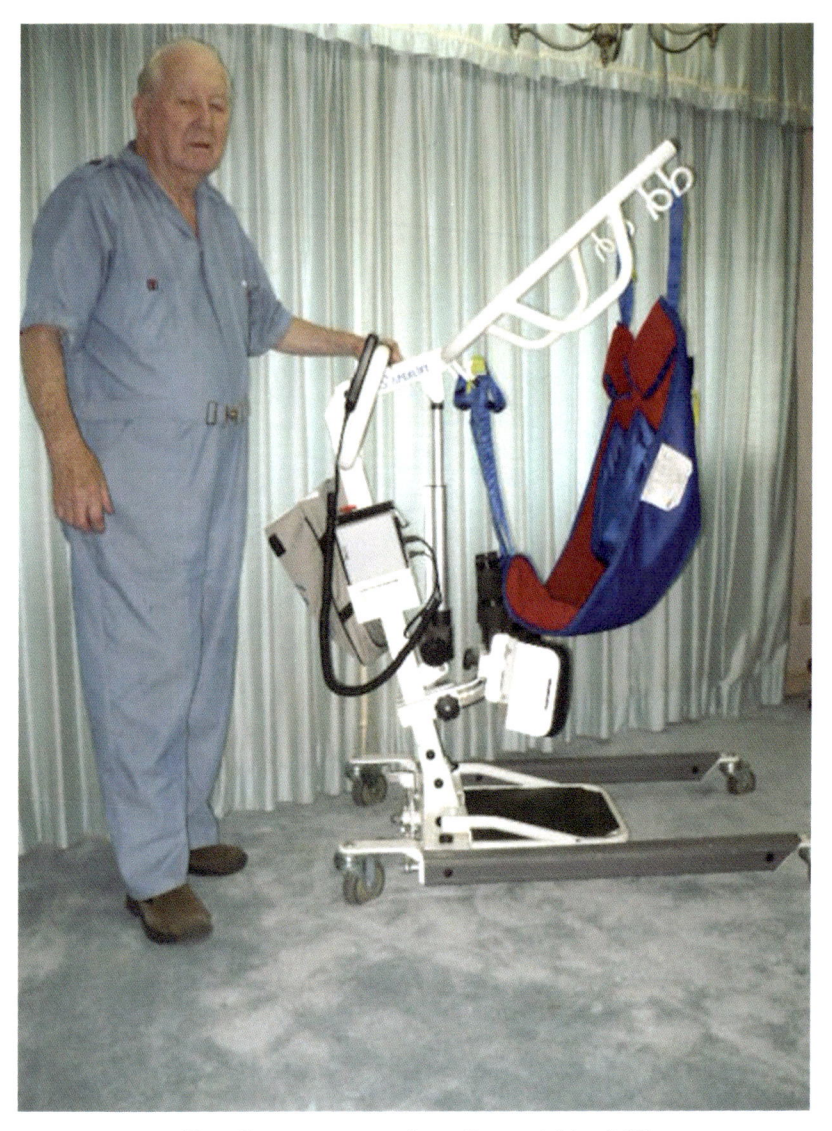

Jim Demonstrating Stand Up Lift

Rest and Comfort

As years went on, Jean became less mobile and slept more; therefore, she spent a lot of time between the bed and chair in the family room. We enjoyed people visiting and every day Ruth (Jean's main hired caregiver) would give her two full body messages and put her limbs through range of motion exercises so her body and her skin stayed as healthy as possible. A few years ago, she had a few pressure sores on her hip and foot, but we conquered them and she had no active sores on her body for the last few years.

When we put Jean to bed, we propped up her legs a bit so that her heels weren't touching the bed and made sure no covers were pushing down on her feet. We also took special care to examine her body so that, if a spot looked like it might be getting weak, we would move her to her other side. These are the things we did to prevent bedsores and we must have done things right because bed sores weren't a problem while Jean was bedridden.

We never were big television fans but we did watch evening news and she seemed to show some response to the activities of the day. I'm sure she didn't remember what was going on but I recall, one time, we were watching the game show "Deal or No Deal". It got a little crucial when one player was asked if he wanted to go on. Jean looked over and pointed and said, "No deal!" So, on occasion, patients have flashbacks that are interesting to observe.

It might also be good to play some music on occasion if it is music the patient enjoys. Sometimes music can bring back memories and certain recognition. *"Jean was always interesting to talk with; she was funny without trying to be funny."* Jim Murr

Keeping in Contact

Mainly, we tried to make sure Jean was engaged, physically and emotionally, when she was awake. Being asleep so much during the day Jean might be awake for five minutes and sleep an hour or she could be awake an hour and sleep five minutes. We just tried to be prepared and the best thing to do is be there for the patient when she awakens. When you finally put the patient to bed in the evening it is the time to do chores.

Anyone caring for a loved one will notice a significant increase in the amount of laundry. Some people make up their minds that they will wash one load each day, the thought being that it's easier to wash one load a day than seven loads once a week. Personally, we did laundry "on the fly" and experienced no build up of dirty laundry.

A few years ago, I moved the washer and dryer up from the lower level; it's nice to have these appliances handy when you have a lot of laundry to do. This made life easier because of not having steps to deal with and also kept us closer to Jean.

Meals

In the morning, we always started with something the children call "gruel." It is nothing more than three tablespoons of bran mixed with yogurt or fruit of some kind and it did allow us to get her pills crushed and mixed into the cereal. In addition she may have had an egg or other breakfast-type item.

For years, Jean had no trouble maintaining her weight and she also had regular bowel movements; otherwise, this might be a big problem for some people. It is very important to observe what is going on with a patient's bowels.

Bowel and bladder issues usually get more difficult as the disease progresses. But if handled in the manner we did, it becomes part of the daily routine and not a major event.

Observing the appearance of the bowel movement will give you information as to what needs to be done to avoid constipation or other bowel problems with the patient. Often adjustment in the patient's diet is all that is necessary. Sometimes medication is called for.

In our experience, medications did not work as well as adjustments in the daily diet. Foods that worked for us included bran, juice, fruit and plenty of liquids.

An exercise program is also important for regular bowel movements. With a patient who is confined to home or is bedridden, perhaps the only option is a range-of-motion exercise done by a caregiver.

It is also good to record the day and time of a patient's bowel movements to help you anticipate the event. When

Jean was no longer able to use the bathroom by herself, I purchased a portable commode which we could move close to her chair or bed.

A caregiver is often able to detect when a patient needs help with toileting and this will prevent accidents. This is the ideal time to use a standup lift if you have one. It is easy to use and the patient can be transferred easily and quickly to the commode.

"During middle stage Alzheimer's, Jim and Jean sat by the fireplace, ate popcorn, and held hands at night when watching TV. In late stage Alzheimer's, they still held hands." Ruth Suttles, Jean's main hired caregiver.

The Comfort Station
By Donna McAndrews

The goal of a family with a loved one who suffers from Alzheimer's is to provide as good a life as possible and for as long as possible . And getting help early is so important (more on this later).

Keeping a loved one with Alzheimer's at home requires family members to remain optimistic and planning for the best outcome: peace and contentment. Avoiding stress for the patient also reduces stress for the family members. Things in our environment known to reduce stress are music, message, aromatherapy, art, physical exercise, pets, meditation and, the all-important, laughter.

Sleep is also of vital importance for the patient and the caregiver. Seven to eight hours at night is ideal and don't rule out naps during the day, whenever possible. This is the surest way to avoid burn-out and becoming run-down. Being as active as possible and eating the healthiest diet possible aid in sleep and overall wellbeing.

Also, keep your social activities and connections, as much as possible. Share with friends and family members to the extent you are able. If you can't go to them, they will come to you. Knowing how families do things, expect them to bring in food to keep up your spirits. Therefore, have a table, or some space, cleared to be able to set up bottles of water, soda, deli sandwiches, fruit and vegetables. People know how to keep things simple when need be. So, a "gathering space" will appear somewhere in your home, well-stocked with comfort foods for all. Take time to enjoy it when you are able.

At Jim and Jean's home, the comfort station appeared in the family room where the couple spent most of their waking hours. In addition to occasional chairs and other comforts you'd look for in a den, this room also had a large table, dining chairs and several large windows which gave a panoramic view of the back yard.

The comfort station is sure to appear in your home, too, whether it is a cozy corner, a counter, a table or a room.

"A doughnut and a cup of coffee work wonders for the caregiver."   Jim Murr

Family room

RAINBOW

...A time for embracing...Eccl 3:5

*It takes both rain and sunshine to make a rainbow.
Author unknown.*

Care Giving
By Jim Murr

We hired Ruth as a companion/caregiver for Jean during Jean's final seven years. Ruth was retired and had nursing home experience and had given home care to other families.

After three days, Ruth and Jean decided to adopt each other, both of them never having had a sister, but always wanting one. They remained devoted to each other for seven years, right until the very night Jean died. It was a perfect fit.

There is a Ruth in your community, too.

Ruth Suttles, daily caregiver for 7 years

September 2009
By Jim Murr

I tried to coax a kiss out of her. She didn't oblige the first time. On the second try, Jean responded. And more than that, the kiss was followed by her most beautiful smile.

The above scenario would not be unusual were it not for the fact that Jean was 88 years of age, married to me, Jim, for 62 years and was at an advanced level of Alzheimer's disease. I chose to care for her in our home where we had lived the past 50 years. In spite of this terrible disease we were happy and at peace.

Following the kiss, I cracked a joke and laughed. Jean laughed right with me. Even though she didn't understand the humor, she hadn't forgotten how to laugh. Another miracle!

"'Yoo-hoo' was our favorite way of calling to each other when at home." Jim Murr

Jean, September 2009, 3 weeks before her death

Ruth was quite a find when it came to caring for my most precious possession—Jean.

Ruth is experienced, well-qualified and calm. Because of Ruth's exceptional hands-on care, Jean never had stiff muscles or other problems associated with being home bound and bed bound.

Jean was Ruth's "sunshine" and had the ability to make Ruth's day with her smile.

In addition to Ruth, three nursing students served at various times, until they graduated. Students are a great resource. Pam, Rene and Meagan were all smart to the point of showing me the correct methods of care giving. Hiring our own help cost less than one-half of what private agencies charge. This I could afford.

My children are all raising families, so I tried to limit using them except for emergency help when I was alone and needed help NOW!

I can't stress enough the importance of consistency of care for the patient. All the caregivers I hired could give body massages, prepare meals, feed Jean at an appropriate pace to avoid choking and administer medicines.

There are qualified nursing students who make good caregivers in your area, also. You can find them. All of our help was recruited through networking, so we always used people we had known for some time.

"Part of it is saving money, but quality of life is the best part." Jim Murr

A Proposal

Our care for Jean while she had Alzheimer's was so successful that we are suggesting that a larger controlled study be made by the medical profession, Medicare or the Alzheimer's Association. The purpose of the study would be to try to reproduce the same results we achieved. If the study produced the same results, this would greatly improve the well-being of the patient, create thousands of new jobs, and keep the sick in the comfort of their home surroundings and save a huge amount of money. Properly controlled, this program could be financed out of funds that are presently being used with relatively poor results. This is a winning program for everyone who is enveloped with care-giving of Alzheimer's patients.

The project would start by selecting a study group. I think Mayo Clinic would be a front-runner for such a study. The patient load should be small enough to be properly monitored and large enough for the results to be meaningful. The patients should be selected soon after they are diagnosed with Alzheimer's and before there is any sign of loneliness or depression. As many friends or relatives as possible should stay in face-to-face contact on a daily basis. This is a major commitment and the majority of the volunteers will soon get down to a few. Fortunately, this is enough but the more the better. This is not a chore for the faint-hearted. There will be some who will not succeed.

The main caregiver should be selected to enforce the home program. Depending on the need, a social worker should be involved at least in the early start-up of the home program. Such a caregiver could very well be a home live-in addition to the family. If a connection is made between the patient and this caregiver you can be quite sure the caregiver will be one of the last people to be forgotten by the patient. In Jean's case, she knew Ruth and me until the end because of seeing us on a daily basis.

Ruth and I took Jean to the doctor for regular check-ups. Getting Jean to the third floor doctor's office was intense labor. A nurse's visit to the home, in most cases, would have done as well, but was not an available service to us at the time.

When Jean came under the umbrella of Hospice care, a nurse would come once a week, or more, if necessary. This service for the patient is desirable for those doing home care. Screening of people providing caregiving of any kind should be thorough. Schooling and continuing education would be a requirement for a yearly certification and license.

The hourly pay rates we used, while not excessive, were reasonable, and allowed us to select very good people. It should be noted that the pay scale would vary from one area to another and is not in the scope of this book to explore in detail.

We kept all employees under a workers' compensation policy, paid all required social security taxes, payroll withholding taxes, and so forth. If an employee worked a split shift, we would work out a travel allowance. All of the above, including the hourly wage, was one-half of what an agency would have charged. If a system such as this could be achieved, a method of bonding the employees could be put in place.

"A peck of common sense is worth a bushel of learning." Author unknown

A Peaceful Passing

The final chapter of Jean's life ended on September 9, 2009. Jean passed on at 7:24 p.m...

About nine hours earlier, she had had a physical by a hospice nurse and showed no sign of a problem; I was gone at the time of Jean's passing.

Ironically, I was visiting a homebound friend when Ruth, who was the caregiver that evening, called to tell me to come quickly. I was only a short distance from home but arrived about three minutes late. Jean had been sleeping and appeared to have died a very peaceful death.

"Death is not extinguishing the light; it is putting out the lamp because dawn has come." Rabindranath Tagore

The picture of the smiling Jean shown earlier in this book was taken three weeks before she died. It shows her usual "waking-up smile" and made the day for me and the caregivers who were lucky enough to catch it. The picture was taken by Marge, a hospice volunteer with many years of care giving experience, and truly a godsend for Jean in her time of need.

There is no place in Heaven too high for nurses and caregivers who do hospice service, whether as a contractor, Medicare worker or volunteer.

"Don't think too far ahead or it's too depressing—so take a day at a time."
Jim Murr

Looking Back at a Special Book

When we had decided to care for Jean at home, I was given a "how-to" book, "Alzheimer's Caregivers", written by Coach Frank Broyles. I admit I did not give the book the time and attention it deserved. We took a day at a time, confident we would reach our goal.

After Jean died on September 9, 2009, I found the coach's book, reread it, and now I can relate to the coach's "game plan" or "play book" as he calls it.

Anyone doing homecare should get their free copy and make it available to the caregivers in your support group. At least a weekly reading of each stage the patient is in would be a good idea. Call it your bible study, if you will. You will thank Coach Broyles.

A Mosaic of Practical Matters

"I am only one, but I am one, I cannot do everything, but I can do something; and what I should do and can do, by the grace of God, I will do."   Edward Everett Hale

Practical Considerations and Finances
By Jim Murr

Bed Rails

When Jean needed help getting in and out of bed, side rails were needed. A set of plastic rails cost one hundred sixty dollars. I was able to make a set of rails for seventeen dollars with piping from Menards and the rails were superior to the costly ready-made rails.

"No one is more ingenious at solving a difficult problem than Jim himself." Donna McAndrews

Shower Rails

When Jean could no longer use a bathtub, the shower was a godsend. However, the shower stall had three glass sides which could not accommodate regular grab bars. I called a medical supply company for help. They did have grab bars that could be installed on glass and they were willing to install two bars for $200 each. Feeling desperate, I decided to order the two bars and asked my daughter to write out a check. She, in turn, had me check another source.

I then recalled watching large glass windows being moved with suction cups that had handles. So, I went to a Harbor Freight Co. store and purchased four suction cup grab bars. Total cost was $26. The lesson learned, of course, is not to buy without checking another source.

"Rushing confuses the patient; take every step slowly."
Jim Murr

Healing Pressure Sores

Because Jean needed to be in bed for long hours, she developed a large pressure sore on one heel and a second one starting on her other heel. With help from Katie, her hospice nurse, we devised a method of elevating her feet and keeping the blanket weight off her feet. Total cost of this solution was ninety seven cents. Thus, at the time of death, Jean had not one active bedsore or pressure sore, in spite of being bed and chair-confined for four years.

"Have courage to be ignorant of a great number of things, in order to avoid the calamity of being ignorant of everything." Author unknown

Work Station

We also installed a work station, which consisted of a wash basin, a bed and a portable commode. This made it convenient for caregivers to serve Jean close to the bed.

Extra Shelving

We emptied an entryway closet, installed shelving and stored all linens, bedding, towels, bathing items, etc. close to the work station.

Hospice Care, Costs and Billing of Hired Employees

I requested a printout of all the hospice care bills for Jean for the 22 months she was on hospice until the time of her death. The total amount I was given was an astounding $194,018.44. This, along with charges for some outpatient visits (care not available at home) came to the grand total of $218,709.38, all paid by Medicare.

Now, hospice homecare consists of a caregiver coming to the patient's home five days a week; holidays and weekends are not included. For Jean's normal care, two hours per call including travel time is a fair estimate. This would increase if Jean was being visited by a nurse and needed help with a special procedure. The nurse came one day a week but was available 24 hours a day, 365 days a year. We used this after-hour service a number of times.

It is a fair estimate that all the Hospice in-home, on-site care giving was 20 hours per week including travel time, or 82 hours per month. If we multiply 82 hours times 22 months, we have 1804 total hours of care for Jean for 22 months. This means that each hour of bedside care cost $107.00 per hour. What's wrong with this picture?

Although the service was always handled professionally, in my opinion, it was limited in scope. Our system of hiring caregivers in order to supplement the Hospice effort cost $18.80 per hour. Thus, we were able to add many comforts and treatments not given to Jean under her Hospice care. No need arose to supplement the weekly nursing care; that part of the program was always handled very well within the limits of our agreement, until an incident occurred toward the end of Jean's life.

No answer had been forthcoming concerning a problem with Jean's leg. This made it necessary for me to take Jean outside the Hospice system for one day. By doing so, I was able to learn of a procedure which worked very well for Jean right up until the end of her life. The leg pain she was having disappeared and she was once again pain free without the use of pain medicine.

Last Twelve Months of Hospice Care

The last twelve months that Jean lived, I paid an additional $30,000 out of pocket which was not covered by Medicare in order to pay for additional help needed for Jean's care.

In addition to the one hour of hospice care five mornings a week, Jean required help with feeding, medicine, exercise and full-body massage, as well as extensive finger movement to prevent her fingers from locking into a curved position; this would have caused her fingernails to grow into the palms of her hands. This latter treatment was very successful.

The above care was given morning and evening, weekends and holidays. She also needed care, of course, getting into bed after toileting. Also, hygiene help was given. In the evening, Jean was given the same type of facial treatment she used to given herself nightly. Thus, at her passing, she still had the peaches and cream complexion she was known to have in her youth.

When Jean could no longer go to the beauty shop for her weekly appointment, I set up a beauty bowl in our heated garage so that the caregivers could do her hair in the style she liked. When looking into the mirror, Jean would smile at the result, regardless of what stage of Alzheimer's she happened to be in at the time.

All this care was possible because Ruth Suttles agreed to work a split shift when she was able and I hired other help as needed.

Stained Glass

...a time for keeping silent, a time for speaking...
Eccl 3:7

    "Never forget you are a part of the people who can be fooled some of the time." Author unknown

Buyer beware

Supplementary Maintenance Income for Home Health Care

In August, 2008, Home Care America, asked me to contact their home office in Yuma, Arizona to see if I'd be interested in obtaining a low-cost maintenance contract for homecare services in our home when needed, for either Jean or myself. I requested more information and a representative came to our home to interview us and explained the program. At the time, Jean had been in hospice for ten months.

He approved Jean's care with their program starting as soon as I purchased it. As we know, hospice care does not completely cover the patient's needs. In Jean's case, a gap of 22 plus hours a day had to be covered by other means.

With the help of our daughters, Susan and Kathy, our caregiver Ruth Suttles, and a variety of employees, plus Marge, a hospice volunteer, we were able to keep in contact with Jean around the clock when she was awake.

My daily input was 20 plus hours a day. This may seem an impossible number but if you consider Jean's 14 to 16 sleeping hours per day, it was very manageable. We added extra help when we knew Jean would be awake and when two people were needed for certain tasks, this system worked out very well.

As Jean entered more advanced stages in the disease, changes were made in employee scheduling and training. In our case, the employees had to train the boss. Since the women we hired were former nursing home workers, this boss was always playing catch up ball. This extra help can be costly, depending on level of care. Personally, I always figured it cost nothing since I was spending only half of what we had put aside for our old age; Jean just got there first.

All this explains why the service offered by Home Health appeared so inviting. Their maintenance program promised to pay the additional costs we were incurring.

The program had a one-time flat rate for a one year maintenance program which started September 9, 2008. It was agreed that I would hire the necessary help, pay for social security benefits, withholding taxes, etc., and bill Home Health at the rate of $18.80 per hour. This was less than half the amount they would expect to pay if help was hired through a local care agency, which their program would normally do. The representative knew Jean was in hospice care since she was in the room with the four of us—Jean, myself, the agent and Renee, one of Jean's caregivers.

Renee agreed to take notes of the meeting. We were both a bit skeptical, so I asked the agent how the company could possibly afford to take on a hospice patient. He said not to worry; she was included because we were married and Jean was covered under my contract and, at any rate, their program costs were covered by a 60 percent grant and other income sources; all funds were handled by Bank of America.

"Problem: A convincing lie sounds just like the truth if you do not know the difference." Jim Murr

We checked with the Better Business Bureau in three different states and none of them had a negative report on Home Health America. The program worked just fine for the first few months and each billing was paid. As soon as my billings exceeded the original start-up fee, they attempted to cancel us.

I continued to bill them each month with no response and the representative I dealt with no longer returned my phone calls. Jean died one day after our contract expired.

Lori Swanson, Attorney General for the State of Minnesota, has started a class action law suit against Home Health America on behalf of the many victims of this scam.

"It is better to suffer wrong than to do it, and happier to sometimes be cheated than not to trust."
Author unknown

BREAKING NEWS: Attorney General Lori Swanson and Assistant Attorney General Nathan Brennaman have settled the class action lawsuit against Home Health America. I have received part of my claim and have accepted it as final settlement. My sincere thanks to all who worked on our behalf. Home Health America has agreed to leave Minnesota and never return. The lowest of the low-lives are out there like vultures ready to pounce on the sick and dying. God help us!

A Final Thought from Jim:
Finding the Proper Help

People have told me they cannot find the proper help for love nor money. I tell them to try **love** and **money.**

A person has to be paid a fair rate in order to survive. Not everyone can give up a paid job and volunteer to work for free.

This may be a great place for Medicare to pay the main caregiver enough to survive and keep the patient out of the nursing home. I think that any such program should be put through a means test where those who can afford to pay their own way will have to do so. This should not become a new entitlement program, i.e. because one is growing old, one should get a check.

In summary, look at the cost differential between delivering care the present way and the way we delivered more quality and quantity at a fraction of the hourly cost.

Will this work in every case? It is doubtful; but, where it works, the patient will benefit. The care givers will also win, and cost will be lowered by billions of dollars for the taxpayers.

"There's nothing wrong with being a self-made man if you don't consider the job finished too soon." Author unknown

My long-time friend, Jerry Petron asked me to share a few of my attempts to help others with Alzheimer's and Alzheimer's caregivers:

Searching for support

Early on I was invited to an Alzheimer's support group meeting at a local health center. It sounded like the type of support I was looking for at the time. I was disappointed in that meeting but went again the next week. The meetings were held in a locked ward which could be reached only by a security elevator.

Now the elevator stopped between floors. While waiting for help to arrive I met the other person on board and discovered that she was going to the same meeting I was. She happened to be the daughter of a friend with whom I had lost contact. The woman was seeking help for her mother, the caregiver for her dad, an Alzheimer's patient and my friend from the past.

The mother was in need of some time away from home in a positive setting. I suggested the young woman and I talk about a trade-off after the meeting. I believed that her dad and I could renew our friendship at his home while her mother, I was sure, would enjoy meeting Jean at our home.

The meeting was led by two nurses from a nearby nursing home who offered no helpful advice except to say they would be there for us. This meant, of course, that the nursing home staff would be happy to take our loved ones in as patients. It was my hope to be able to talk to the young woman I met on the elevator in the hope of working out a beneficial arrangement for the two of us and our loved ones.

But, as the meeting broke up, the woman went directly to one of the nurses and I heard the end of their conversation. The nurse was promising to be at her parents' home at eight o'clock the next morning to take Dad to the nursing home.

A few short weeks later I read my friend's name in the obituaries.

A caring offer: an "A+ for effort"

As I heard of friends or relatives with Alzheimer's problems, I would contact them with the following offer: I would buy lunch and talk about how things were working for Jean and me. I did buy several lunches but no one I invited attempted to follow my care program that Jean and I had been using with excellent results. I give myself an A plus rating for my effort and another A plus rating for being the world's most unconvincing teacher!

The majority of the patients and caregivers I spoke with are either dead or in nursing homes or other care today. Jean outlived all of the patients and some of the caregivers. Not one of them took my advice to start care early and determinedly. I'm certain that not one of them died at home in their own bed with a smile each day, as Jean did.

My advice was to start as soon as possible to hire a part time companion for as many hours a day as needed to replace the main caregiver when necessary. The hours would vary depending on the needs of the patient due to the ever-changing stages of the disease. Most people responded that it would be too costly (as though twelve dollars an hour was too much money to help maintain your greatest asset.)

I learned that before long guilt, hopelessness, finances and other problems would soon overwhelm people. The result was a higher cost in both money and the need for more human resources than could be provided at home, requiring a trip to the nursing home. Now stress and guilt really start to take a toll. My advice to new caregivers was to no avail but still worthy of the trying.

I had one big advantage not available to all new caregivers— Ruth, Jean's early companion. Because of Ruth's earlier experiences as a caregiver of Alzheimer's patients, she was able to predict with certainty what to expect as Jean moved through each new phase.

I believe that many thousands of Ruth's could be recruited to fill this crucial need. Ruth stated early on that

Jean would never forget me and how right she was! One more rewarding reason to hang in until the end.

The Caregiver
By Donna McAndrews

"This story is not about me," said Jim. "It's all been possible because of the team; it's about us."

That said, we still need to shed some light on the man that is Jim.

Considering all his lifetime accomplishments, and "high intellect" to quote his daughters, another man might actually have become "uppity", said a friend of Jim's. Jim, however, remains down-to-earth to the extreme.

Imagine a man like this caring for his wife with Alzheimer's for more than a decade at home when, very late in her illness, he took the time to throw a birthday party for a 12-year old friend, "because she had never had a birthday party."

If you engage Jim in conversation, you'll find he has an interesting and home-spun common sense approach to almost every aspect of life. Self-effacing, soft-spoken and sincere, the sparkle in the eyes and the welcome smile cannot be missed.

While running a successful business for several decades, Jim's goal was not to be a "bossy" boss. "People do a better job if you let them be," he said.

In addition to running his business, Jim also served on the City Council, the Housing Authority Board and a high-rise board, to name a few.

When it comes to problem-solving, it is hard to imagine one more ingenious than Jim himself. At the age of 86, Jim is still going steady and strong.

Jim Murr relaxing at home 2010

Jean's Greatest Gift

In short, there are three things that last: faith, hope and love; and the greatest of these is love." 1 Cor. 13:13

So, I thank you, Jean, for the greatest gift: Love. Taking care of you has been my way to return part of the love you showered upon me and so many others throughout all the years.

"*Love is, above all, the gift of oneself.*" Jean Anouih

Jean's Favorite Hymn*

Jesus loves me, this I know, for the bible tells me so. Little ones to him belong; they are weak but He is strong. Yes, Jesus loves me; Yes Jesus loves me; Yes Jesus loves me, the bible tells me so. Jesus loves me, He will stay, close beside me all the way. When at last I come to die, He will take me home on high. Yes, Jesus loves me; Yes, Jesus loves me; Yes, Jesus loves me, the bible tells me so.

*Sung at Jean's funeral service at the request of Jean's Hospice Chaplain, Norman Belland, who often sang to Jean when she was ill.

Memorable Quotes

A.D. will affect one in ten Americans over the age of sixty-five. *"The 10 Best Questions for Living with Alzheimer's; Simon and Shuster; 2008*

Over nine million adult Americans provided 8.4 billion hours of unpaid care to people with A.D. in 2007 according to the Alzheimer's Association. Added to this are more than 52 million family caregivers in the U.S. This figure is expected to increase by 85 percent before 2050 as the boomer generation ages.

"As of 2008, there were over 52 million informal, unpaid caregivers in the U.S., with 59 to 75 percent being women, and helping patients with bathing, dressing, eating, toileting and other tasks." Dede Bonner, P.H.D...

"Your brain is more complex than any organ…no two brains are alike." Dede Bonner, P.H.D.

"It would be good for all of us to focus on the positive, the true, the things that really last, on character, humor, commitment, and love and on the happy memories…" Nancy Reagan in writing about her husband, President Ronald Reagan, an Alzheimer's patient.

"If you don't like something, change it. If you can't change it, change your attitude." Maya Angelou

"We cannot do everything at once; but we can do something at once." Ralph Waldo Emerson

"God has given us two hands—one to receive with and the other to give with. We are not cisterns made for hoarding; we are channels made for sharing." Billy Graham

"To the man in us, time is quantity; to the God in us, it is quality." Author unknown

"Alzheimer's disease is difficult to diagnose. Even after diagnosis, no one is certain it is actually A.D. Only after death, when autopsy is done, can doctors be sure. A free autopsy will be provided and paid for by the Alzheimer's Association. It is believed it is worthwhile to have this done because it may help Alzheimer's patients in the future by

giving researchers valuable information."
Jim Murr

"Just about the time you think you can make both ends meet, somebody moves the ends." Pansey Penner

"If I keep a green bough in my heart, the singing bird will come." Chinese Proverb"

"Ten million Americans currently need some form of longterm care, either at home, or in a nursing home or care facility." Dede Bonner in *"The 10 Best Questions for Living with Alzheimer's"*; Simon and Schuster; 2008.

"Keep in mind there is a high rate of medication errors in nursing homes and residential care, not to mention neglect and abuse." Therese Everson

"On average Alzheimer's patients live from seven to ten years after a diagnosis, with some living up to twenty years." Dede Bonner, P.H.D.

"The main thing is not how long you're on the planet, but the quality you have while you're here." Clint Eastwood

"Life is 10% what you make it and 90% how you take it." Washington Irving

"The number of unpaid caregiver in the United States tops 65 million…and 1/3 of those are men." Gail Sheehy in AARP Magazine; May/June 2010

"The roughly $85,000 a year in nursing home costs, expected to rise by at least six percent every year, makes keeping a relative at home desirable from a financial perspective but, more important, the patient is calmer and less confused at home" Donna McAndrews.

"I've learned that people will forget what you said, people will forget what you did, but people will never forget how you made them feel." Maya Angelou

"When I was younger, I could remember anything, whether it happened or not." Mark Twain

"Old age is the most unexpected of all the things that can happen to a man." Leon Trotsky

"Dying is as natural as being born." Author unknown

"We got unique results out of a unique effort." Jim Murr

"It is not the years in your life that count, but the life in your years." Abraham Lincoln

"You matter to the last moment of your life and we will do all we can not only to help you die peacefully, but to live until you die."
Dame Cicely Saunders, Founder of First Hospice

The First and Last Extra Mile
By Jim Murr

Jean and I were fortunate to have three family members who were there from day one for many of Jean's health problems and who stayed involved until she made a full recovery. Daughters Susan and Kathy always amazed me in the way they could smooze the hospital staff and thus get the very best care and attention for Jean. Of course, Jean herself was very good at connecting with staff because she genuinely liked everyone.

When Jean moved temporarily to a rehab center, the daughters would be there and make sure she had a personal companion with her twenty-four hours a day. Either they stayed or found a replacement. They would help with bringing Jean home and continued until full recovery was made. This might be up to six weeks of recovery in a wheelchair and also turned out successfully.

The oldest granddaughter, Amber, a nurse, would regularly travel with her two children from north of St. Paul to the Murr house south of town and share a meal she would pick up on the way. The grandkids were at a very active age, so were entertaining for us.

Early on, Kathy would bring her two children every Sunday after church and her husband Frank would cook a gourmet meal that would usually last us halfway through the week. All these good times are not soon forgotten.

Thank you from Mom and Dad

Coauthor, Donna McAndrews, is a freelance writer whose previous works include biographies, histories, spiritual books and articles, and public affairs reporting. Donna is a widow with six adult children and sixteen grandchildren and resides in Inver Grove Heights, MN.

**To purchase a copy of this book,
or for more information,
Contact our web site:
livinghappilywithalzheimers.com**